Cane Toad

The World's Biggest Toad

by Leon Gray

Consultant: Dr. Kenneth L. Krysko
Senior Biological Scientist, Division of Herpetology
Florida Museum of Natural History, University of Florida

BEARPORT
PUBLISHING

New York, New York

Credits

Cover and TOC, © Art_man/Shutterstock; 4–5, © Ocean/Corbis; 6–7, © Kathie Atkinson/Auscape/ardea.com; 8, © Jean Paul Ferrero/ardea.com; 9, © Michael & Patricia Fogden/Minden Pictures/FLPA; 10, © Konrad Wothe/Minden Pictures/FLPA; 12, © kaarsten/Shutterstock; 13, © Rolf Nussbaumer/imagebroker/Corbis; 14, © ChameleonsEye/Shutterstock; 15, © Jack Picone/Alamy; 16–17, © Piotr Naskrecki/Minden Pictures/FLPA; 17, © Auscape/ardea.com; 18, © blickwinkel/Alamy; 19, © Pete Oxford/Minden Pictures/FLPA; 20, © David Gray/Reuters/Corbis; 21, © John Carnemolla/Shutterstock; 22L, © Pete Oxford/Minden Pictures/FLPA; 22C, © Jacqueline Abromeit/Shutterstock; 22R, © Steven Russell Smith Photos/Shutterstock; 23TL, © Tom C. Amon/Shutterstock; 23TR, © kaarsten/Shutterstock; 23BL, © Jean Paul Ferrero/ardea.com; 23BR, © Paul Broadbent/Shutterstock.

Publisher: Kenn Goin
Senior Editor: Joyce Tavolacci
Creative Director: Spencer Brinker
Photo Researcher: Calcium Creative

Library of Congress Cataloging-in-Publication Data in process at time of publication (2013)
Library of Congress Control Number: 2012039495
ISBN-13: 978-1-61772-727-6 (library binding)

For more information, write to Bearport Publishing Company, Inc.,
45 West 21st Street, Suite 3B, New York, New York 10010. Printed in the United States of America.

10 9 8 7 6 5 4 3 2 1

Contents

A Giant Toad

The cane toad is the biggest toad in the world.

One of these **amphibians** can grow to the size of a soccer ball.

Cane toads grow up to nine inches (22.9 cm) long. They can weigh up to five pounds (2.3 kg).

common frog

cane toad

Hungry Hunters

Cane toads are big eaters.

They will hunt and eat almost anything they can catch and swallow.

Insects are their favorite food.

They love to eat beetles, honeybees, ants, and crickets.

However, they also eat larger creatures such as snakes, frogs, birds, and small furry animals.

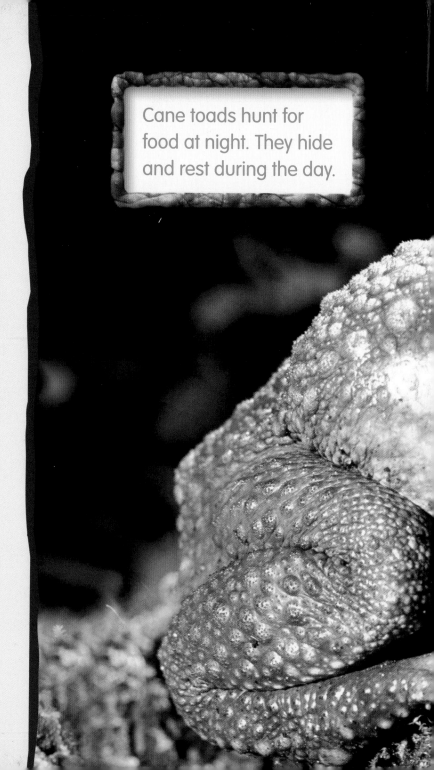

Cane toads hunt for food at night. They hide and rest during the day.

small
opossum

Powerful Poison

Even though they are very large, cane toads are hunted by other animals.

Crocodiles, hawks, and large snakes are some of their enemies.

However, any animal that tries to eat a cane toad will get a nasty surprise.

The big toad can squirt or ooze a milky white **poison** from behind its head.

The powerful poison can burn or blind the attacker—and even kill it.

poison

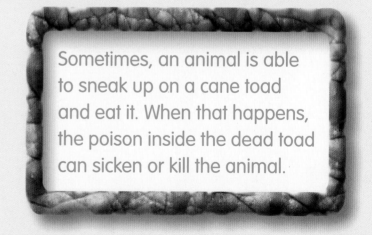

Sometimes, an animal is able to sneak up on a cane toad and eat it. When that happens, the poison inside the dead toad can sicken or kill the animal.

snake

Where in the World?

Cane toads live in warm, wet places.

At one time, they lived only in parts of North, Central, and South America.

During the late 1800s and early 1900s, however, people brought the giant toads to other places.

They thought that the toads would eat beetles that were destroying farmers' crops.

The main crop that people wanted the cane toad to protect was **sugar cane**. That is how the big amphibian got its name.

Cane Toads Around the World

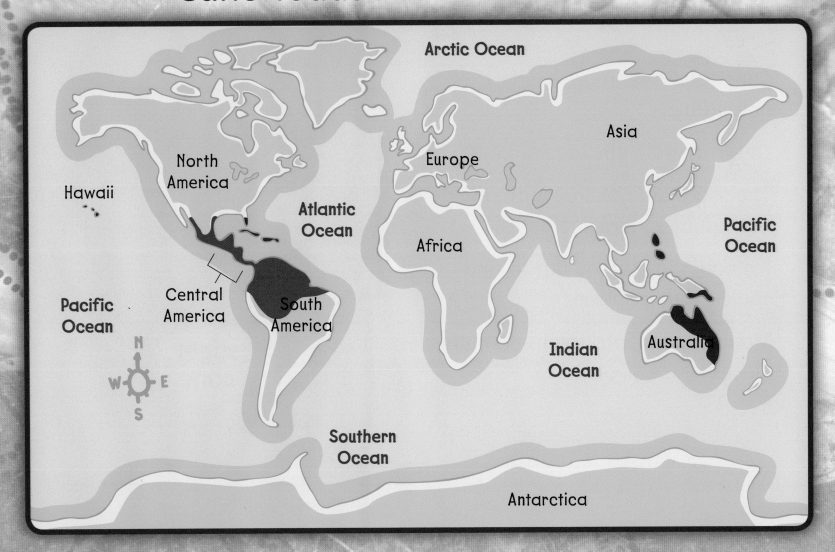

Arctic Ocean

Asia

North America

Europe

Hawaii

Atlantic Ocean

Pacific Ocean

Africa

Pacific Ocean

Central America

South America

Indian Ocean

Australia

N W E S

Southern Ocean

Antarctica

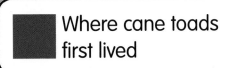 Where cane toads first lived

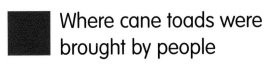 Where cane toads were brought by people

11

Spreading Out

Cane toads were supposed to help farmers.

Unfortunately, the idea did not work.

The toads did not stay in the hot, sunny sugar cane fields.

Instead, they spread out to find cooler, shadier places.

Many hopped into towns and other places where people live.

sugar cane

The cane toads also left the sugar cane fields to find food. That's because the beetles stayed on the top of the tall cane plants. As a result, the toads could not jump high enough to eat the beetles.

Toad Overload

In Australia, cane toads have spread more quickly than anywhere else.

Many cane toads show up in people's yards and do not leave.

They eat pet food from bowls that have been left outside.

Because of their poison, they sicken the dogs and cats that try to attack them.

Cane toads harm wild animals, too. They eat so much food that some animals, such as skinks and other lizards, do not have enough to eat.

skink

15

From Eggs to Tadpoles

Like most amphibians, cane toads start their lives in the water as tiny eggs.

A female toad lays up to 35,000 eggs at one time!

After about three days, **tadpoles** hatch from the eggs.

The baby toads look like little fish.

The have long tails and no legs.

eggs

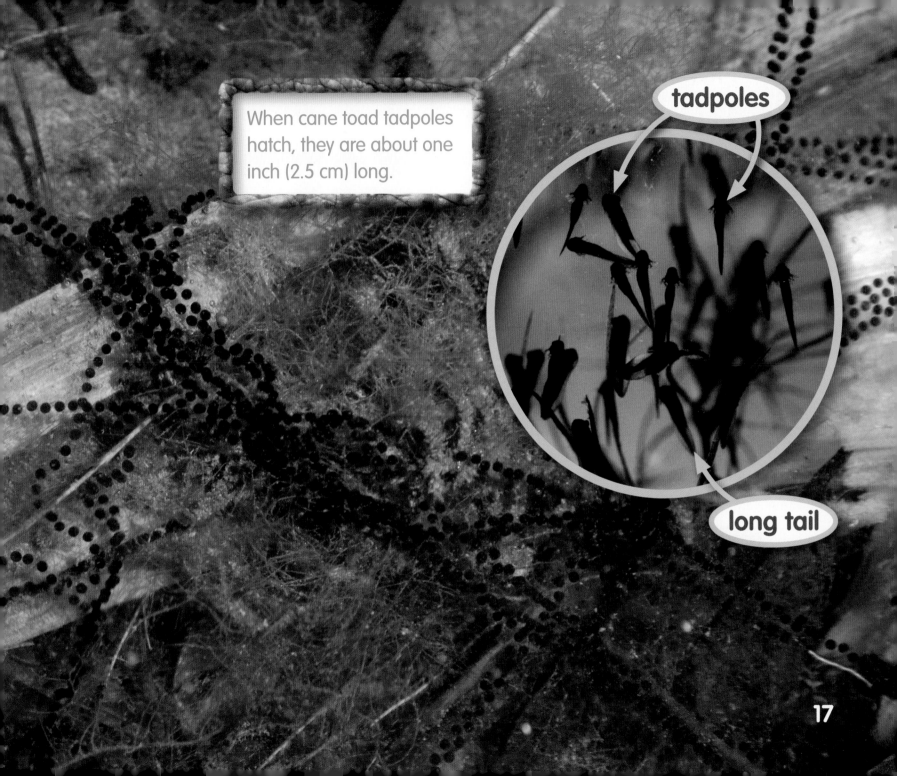

When cane toad tadpoles hatch, they are about one inch (2.5 cm) long.

tadpoles

long tail

17

Tiny Toadlets

A cane toad tadpole lives in the water for up to 60 days.

It eats underwater plants with its tiny peg-like teeth.

Over time, its legs grow, and its tail disappears.

The tiny toadlet looks like its parents and is now ready to leave the water.

At first, toadlets are about two inches (5 cm) long. In about a year, they are fully grown.

tadpoles

young
cane toad

19

Looking for Answers

People in Australia are trying to reduce the number of cane toads.

Some people take the toads' eggs out of the water to keep them from hatching.

Others have fenced off ponds to keep the huge toads from laying eggs in them.

So far, these actions have not made a big difference.

Australians still need to find ways to stop this big toad from becoming an even bigger problem.

captured cane toad

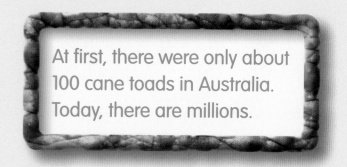

At first, there were only about 100 cane toads in Australia. Today, there are millions.

More Big Toads

Cane toads belong to a group of animals called amphibians. All amphibians are cold-blooded and most start their lives in the water. Most amphibians move to dry land when they grow up. Others stay in or near water.

Here are three more big toads.

Rococo Toad

The rococo toad is almost as big as the cane toad. It can grow up to 8.5 inches (21.6 cm) long.

Colorado River Toad

Another large toad is the Colorado River toad. It can reach a length of 7 inches (17.8 cm).

American Toad

The American toad lives in the eastern United States and can grow up to 4 inches (11.4 cm) long.

Cane Toad
9 inches/22.9 cm

Rococo Toad
8.5 inches/21.6 cm

Colorado River Toad
7 inches/17.8 cm

American Toad
4 inches/11.4 cm

Glossary

amphibians
(am-FIB-ee-uhnz)
animals that have
a backbone and
live part of their
lives in water and
part on land

sugar cane
(SHUG-ur KAYN)
a plant that is
grown and used
to make sugar

poison
(POI-zuhn)
a substance that
can harm or kill
animals

tadpoles
(TAD-polz)
small, young toads
that lack legs and
live in water before
they become
adults

Index

Read More

Schuetz, Kari. *Toads (Blastoff! Readers: Backyard Wildlife).* Minneapolis, MN: Bellwether Media (2012).

Sweeney, Alyse. *Toads (Pebble Plus: Amphibians).* Mankato, MN: Capstone Press (2010).

Trueit, Trudi Strain. *Frogs and Toads (Backyard Safari).* New York: Marshall Cavendish (2012).

Learn More Online

To learn more about cane toads, visit
www.bearportpublishing.com/EvenMoreSuperSized